LYDIA MARCHANT

Lydia Marchant studied MA Writing for Stage and Broadcast Media at the Royal Central School of Speech and Drama. She is a member of the Writing Squad and has taken part in writers' programmes at Soho Theatre, Hampstead Theatre, Leeds Playhouse, National Theatre and Royal Court.

In 2019 she was selected for the BBC's Writers' Academy, led by John Yorke, and she has since written for *Holby City*, *Casualty* and *EastEnders*.

Mumsy is her first full-length play. Her other theatre credits include *Defiance*, *Leftovers*, *After Party* (Hull Truck Theatre); *Changing Rooms* (Paines Plough); *Split* (Separate Doors/Derby Theatre/Chichester Festival Theatre); *Spark* (Pilot Theatre); *Lost and Found* (York Theatre Royal); *Beach Body Ready* (The Roaring Girls/Pleasance); *Park Life* (Silent Uproar); *The Dancing Dead*, *Superhero Society* (Middle Child).

Her podcast credits include *British Scandal* (Wondery) and *The Last Soviet* (Samizdat Audio).

Lydia Marchant

MUMSY

NICK HERN BOOKS
London
www.nickhernbooks.co.uk

A Nick Hern Book

Mumsy first published in Great Britain as a paperback original in 2023 by Nick Hern Books Limited, The Glasshouse, 49a Goldhawk Road, London W12 8QP

Mumsy copyright © 2023 Lydia Marchant

Lydia Marchant has asserted her right to be identified as the author of this work

Cover artwork by Hull Truck Theatre

Designed and typeset by Nick Hern Books, London
Printed in Great Britain by Mimeo Ltd, Huntingdon, Cambridgeshire PE29 6XX

A CIP catalogue record for this book is available from the British Library

ISBN 978 1 83904 213 3

Mumsy was first performed at Hull Truck Theatre on 2 March 2023, with the following cast:

SOPHIE	Jessica Jolleys
RACHEL	Nicola Stephenson
LINDA	Sue Kelvin

Director	Zoë Waterman
Set and Costume Designer	Bronia Housman
Lighting Designer	Jessica Brigham
Sound Designer	Hattie North
Casting Director	Liv Barr
Casting Assistant	Francesca Tennant
Voice Coach	Elspeth Morrison
Producer	Adam Pownall
Production Manager	Paul Veysey
Assistant Producer	Zoe Walker
Company Stage Manager	Shona Wright
Deputy Stage Manager	Edward Salt
Assistant Stage Manager	Danielle Harris
Wardrobe Supervisor	Sian Thomas
Master Carpenter	Chris Bewers
Carpenter	Daniel Lewis
Scenic Art	Sarah Feasey

Acknowledgements

I'd like to say a massive thanks to Mark Babych and Tom
Saunders at Hull Truck Theatre for seeing something in the very
rough first draft and giving me everything I possibly needed to
shape the play into something I'm really proud of. I'm also
really grateful to former Hull Truck staff including Tom
Bellerby, Jill Adamson, Morgan Sproxton and Nick Lane, for all
the support and advice they've given me on my journey, and for
helping me believe I could be a writer.

I'd like to thank director Zoë Waterman, actors Jessica Jolleys,
Nicola Stephenson and Sue Kelvin and the whole creative team
for bringing this thing from my head to life in the most
fantastic way.

Also huge thanks to Josie Morley and Kate Hampson for all
their help developing the characters of Sophie and Rachel. And
thank you to all the brilliant mums I spoke to – and to the Act 3
group at Hull Truck for helping me shape the character of Linda
(and hopefully get the 1970s pop culture references right!).

I'd like to thank Leeds Playhouse, in particular Jacqui Honess-
Martin and Charley Miles, and staff from MA Writing for Stage
and Broadcast Media at Royal Central School of Speech and
Drama for all their help shaping the early drafts.

Finally, massive thanks to my mum (without whose support this
play just wouldn't exist) and my boyfriend Tom for reading the
drafts that were too crap to show anyone else and to my family
for all their support and not telling me to get a proper job.

L.M.

For my mum, granny and grandma

Characters

SOPHIE, *twenty-two*
RACHEL, *forty*
LINDA, *sixty-one*

Notes

The setting is the living / dining / kitchen area of a one-bedroom flat in West Hull, England.

The staging of the play is totally open to interpretation – the stage directions invoke the literal world of the characters, but don't demand literal staging.

At the time of writing businesses are closing all the time (RIP Topshop), so brand names can be changed if no longer relevant. As can rates of pay.

Words in [square brackets] are unspoken.

This text went to press before the end of rehearsals and so may differ slightly from the play as performed.

ACT ONE

Scene One

Five Weeks Pregnant

Time: 9 p.m.

Rachel's one-bedroom flat.

Girlie night.

SOPHIE. Okay, so… em… okay. Basically, a few weeks ago
I meet this lad on Tinder –

RACHEL. You? On Tinder? Way to go, Soph!

SOPHIE. Thanks, yeah. So –

RACHEL. Didn't think you had it in you.

SOPHIE. So I meet his lad. And he's… yeah. So we decide to
go on a date.

RACHEL. Where'd he take you?

SOPHIE. Um… Wetherspoon's.

RACHEL. Spoons?!

SOPHIE. He said it's two-for-one chicken on a Wednesday.

RACHEL. God, I'd of thought I brought you up with more
self-worth than Spoons, Soph.

Nando's at the very least.

Know what? I don't think you're beyond aiming for Pizza
Express.

SOPHIE. Thanks, Mum.

RACHEL. So, go on, what's he like?

SOPHIE. Like? Well, I ask for a pint of Amstel, and he comes back with a Bombay Sapphire.

'More ladylike' he says.

RACHEL. 'Ladylike'? Shoulda got that Bombay Sapphire, 'n' chucked it in his pig-ugly face. I would.

SOPHIE. Know you would.

RACHEL. So, a prick then?

SOPHIE. Well… yeah. Like through the whole thing he's banging on about his ''21 Plate Mazda Sport'. His job driving the forklifts for the garlic bread factory over the river. His dreams of managing the people what drive the forklifts for the garlic bread factory over the river. Dunt even ask my surname…

Little top-up?

RACHEL. Cheers yeah. Just a tad.

Er, more than that.

Not a goer then?

SOPHIE. Well, um, first ten minutes of the date I'm like, definitely not. But then…

RACHEL. Oh, Sophie.

SOPHIE. He just seems so sure, you know? That it's gonna happen. And part of me dunt wanna offend him. And maybe it's the gin but the whole time we're sat there, and then when we're on the bus back to his. It's like I'm stood outside myself going, 'Come on, Sophie, do you really wanna do this?'

But it's happening, you know?

RACHEL. So?

SOPHIE. So we go back to his. And…

We kinda start, you know. And then I'm like, 'You got any – '

RACHEL. Johnnies.

That's my girl.

SOPHIE. And he gets out this box of extra-large ones.

But then I look at his Thing and I'm thinking, 'no way', you know? 'Cause it's... [tiny.]

RACHEL. Ah, button mushroom.

SOPHIE. But I can't... I mean, I don't wanna say anything...

So anyway, we... And it's... And he finishes and pulls out and I'm like, 'Er, what you done with the, you know... condom?' Thinking, 'Oh my God has he been stealthing me?'

But he's like 'I dunno! I honestly dunno!'

So we start searching, and eventually... oh God... eventually, we um, we work out it's still...

RACHEL. What?

SOPHIE. Can I get you any more, you know, wine or...?

RACHEL. Soph.

SOPHIE. Eventually we work out it's still... inside.

RACHEL....

SOPHIE. And I'm literally fishing round in there for ages, but it's like it's been sucked right, you know, up. So I'm like right – going straight to A&E. Having this thing removed, morning-after pill –

RACHEL. And a full examination. You hant got a clue where that little thing's been.

SOPHIE. But then I look at my watch... six in the morning. I've gotta be at work in forty-five minutes and I'm in the middle of like... Grimsby.

RACHEL. Sophie.

SOPHIE. So I go into Bright Sparks, all smiles and 'Hands up who wants to sing the clap-clap good morning song.' All the while thinking, 'Oh my God, bet he's given me the clap-clap.'

Finally gets to half-six. But as I'm leaving Helen –

RACHEL. Ugh, Snotty Helen.

SOPHIE. Helen asks me to write up a Next Steps report 'cause Leo put three blocks together unaided. And I can't turn round and say 'Sorry, I've gotta go down Family Planning 'cause there's a Durex Real Feel probably wrapped round my Fallopian tubes and I've almost definitely got chlamydia.'

Not if I wanna keep my DBS.

So by the time I get out, eight-fifteen. Conifer House's only gone and closed. This point I'm just shattered.

End up stood with my leg up on the bath, poking round in there with the other end of a toothbrush till the thing just plops out.

RACHEL. Oh my God, Sophie. I can't believe you –

SOPHIE. Mum, I'm pregnant.

Scene Two

Five Weeks Pregnant

Two-ish minutes later.

Beat.

RACHEL. No.

No.

No no no no no.

This int happening.

Not now. Not now.

This is why you…

Gestures at the wine.

'Fancy a girls' night, Mam.' And then BOOM blindside me.

I'm missing 'Legs, Bums and Tums' for this.

SOPHIE. I thought you'd be happy!

Beat.

RACHEL. No...

You're not thinking of keeping it?

SOPHIE. What?

RACHEL *finishes the bottle*.

RACHEL. Twenty-five Slimming World SYNS. Thanks, Soph. Thanks a lot.

SOPHIE. It's weird like... Growing up I always kinda, pictured I'd be this age. As in – this exact age. When I had a baby.

RACHEL. This int you... This int what you want. You're still... All them poncey courses you're doing. The one where they twat about in woods.

SOPHIE. Forest Education Leadership.

RACHEL. And where you have 'em all running round with little saws and hammers.

SOPHIE. Level Three Risky Play. I can still do all that. And the learning support degree.

RACHEL. Ugh, twenty-seven grand for a piece of paper what says you can do the job you've already been doing for six years.

SOPHIE. None of that has to stop just because I'm having a baby.

RACHEL. A baby? Oh darling, you have no idea.

SOPHIE. I love my job. I really love my job. I do. But, well... There's a part of me... like, when I see Helen with her Oscar.

RACHEL. Shoulda known Snotty Helen'd have summat to do with this.

SOPHIE. When I see her with Oscar. It's like there's a part of me what's, I dunno, missing. This like, ache.

RACHEL. Then get a bob. Or a nipple piercing. Not a blooming baby!

SOPHIE. Mum!

Look, all I know is, when I took that pregnancy test I was shitting myself. Hand was shaking – took me three attempts to hold it under the pee. Thinking 'I'm not ready for this. I'm not ready.'

Then I went outside, lit a cig, and the minute I saw the two blue lines I just… spat it out. Dint even think about it. Binned the full packet.

RACHEL. So?

SOPHIE. It's a sign.

RACHEL. It's a waste of twelve-pound-forty.

SOPHIE. It's a sign I really wanna do this.

RACHEL. Yeah and I 'wanna be' sunbathing topless on a beach in Ibiza.

But right now I'm working my arse off – teaching assistant, dinner lady, school bog cleaner… Getting thirty minutes off, eight while six and only just covering my rent.

Just 'cause you 'wanna do' summat dunt mean it's the right time.

You're twenty-two.

SOPHIE. Four years older than you was!

RACHEL. And I'm guessing, you and this bloke.

SOPHIE. It's nowt to do with him! I mean, I'm not being… But literally all he did was –

RACHEL. Blow his load. I geddit. But that means you're on your own.

SOPHIE. Like you was.

And Nan.

RACHEL. But what about money? Sophie, your job int exactly secure.

SOPHIE. Says you! Oh my God, Mum. You went through, what? Seven jobs in six months? Before you got pregnant.

RACHEL. Yeah, well, it was a different time.

SOPHIE. The beauty therapy place. Where you got fired after two and a half hours.

RACHEL. Harder that it looks, that sorta thing. You put the wrong cream in the wrong place and folk get burned.

SOPHIE. I just mean like, you was way less prepared than me. I've got a career.

RACHEL. A 'career'! God's sake, Sophie, you're on a zero-hour contract! On what? Nine-pound-eighteen an hour?

SOPHIE. Yeah… well… I'm up to thirty-five, forty hours most weeks now. And Helen says I'm really going places. Says the minute a level-two position comes up –

RACHEL. She's been saying that for years, Soph.

SOPHIE. Well it's still more than you had.

And you, you know, did really good, with me. Dint you? Really good.

Like, I really thought… you know, out of everyone, I really thought you'd understand.

Beat.

God, you don't think I can do this, do you?

RACHEL. I aren't saying…

SOPHIE. When we did infant simulator dolls in practical assessment – we had to take home, feed, change, get up in the night with them. And I got the highest mark in the whole entire –

RACHEL. I know you can play with bloody dolls, Soph. I'm the one what had to go round all them charity shops every Saturday getting your Baby Borns real babygrows.

SOPHIE. Mum, no, that int –

RACHEL. Pretending they was real. Asking the bloke in Pizza Hut for a high chair. You – tryna breastfeed one o'them in the middle o'the Transport Museum!

SOPHIE. Ugh, why do you always have to be…? Ugh.

RACHEL. Being a mum int playing with dolls, Soph. Dolls don't grow out of onesies in a fortnight or shit their way through fifty nappies a week.

SOPHIE. I know that! How can you say I don't know that? I'm a childcare professional! I work in a nursery!

RACHEL. With kids whose parents can afford to live in Kirk Ella.

SOPHIE. Okay. I get it.

RACHEL. Really don't think you –

SOPHIE. It's because I've never been good at anything.

RACHEL. For God's sake.

SOPHIE. In school. Last kid in the year to get a pen licence –

RACHEL. Yeah I really think it's time to let that go.

SOPHIE. With mates as well. Always the third wheel. Seeing on Facebook, the birthday tea at Frankie and Benny's no one wanted me at.

RACHEL. You was just oversensitive. Still are.

SOPHIE. Molly Jordan… Molly Jordan saying… telling me to, you remember, 'go slit my wrists' on Ask FM.

RACHEL. Always taking things to heart.

SOPHIE. But thing is, when I got into college, got the apprenticeship, and when they kept me on after…

It just clicked. I'm actually good at this. Working with kids, caring for them, understanding them, bringing them on. I'm really bloody good.

RACHEL. Soph –

SOPHIE. And last night, when I took the test, I got the same, feeling. So excited – couldn't breathe. Just knew –

Really knew –

I could be a good mum.

RACHEL. Darling, you'll be a good mum at thirty, thirty-five, when you're financially stable. They're freezing eggs like fish fingers these days. Wait to sixty. Be a good mum then!

SOPHIE. No.

RACHEL. Sophie…

SOPHIE. I said no. I'm proper excited about this baby. Couldn't sit still for like five hours after I took the test. Just paced round and round and round my room. Like… tingling.

Knowing this baby was growing inside me.

So I um… I made –

RACHEL. What?

SOPHIE. A spreadsheet. Like a budget.

RACHEL. Soph…

SOPHIE. Cash-flow of what I've got coming in at the moment. And I'll have my maternity pay – ninety per cent of my average earnings.

Estimates of the expenses. Clothes, nappies and things. Savings as well – twenty-five pound a month, so baby and me can afford a place of our own.

And, you know, it's actually doable. I really think, if I'm careful, I'll have enough left over for a Deluxe Snuggle Pod.

RACHEL. What?

SOPHIE. Aw, Mum, it's the best! Co-sleeper cot for beside the bed. Comes with reflux support, three-hundred-and-sixty-degree air-flow system…

RACHEL *opens another bottle.*

So yeah. I'm gonna…

'Cause I've thought this through, haven't I? I've made a spreadsheet.

And you know statistically I'm the best age to have a baby? Like biologically.

Fertility starts decreasing after twenty-four. I read that.

What if I never get a chance again?

I really think I can do this. You can say what you like, but I'm an adult, it's up to me.

Beat.

So, yeah, um Mum… Can I move back in with you?

Fuck.

Scene Three

Six Weeks Pregnant

Time: 7 p.m.

RACHEL*'s setting up the sofa bed.*

SOPHIE*'s bringing in two bags.*

Then another two.

And another two…

RACHEL (*forced*). Must of had a job fitting all this in that box room.

SOPHIE. Not really.

RACHEL. Is that… seven dressing gowns? Dint realise I gave birth to a sloth.

SOPHIE. We had a 'no heating' rule.

Issy caved once 'cause her pants wouldn't dry and we made her scrape the mould off the shower with a toothbrush.

RACHEL. Right.

SOPHIE. Thanks again, you know, for this.

RACHEL. Least I get all my stolen Tupperware back.

RACHEL gestures to a bag full of Tupperware.

SOPHIE. Mum, I'm being serious. Like it's nice, us doing this together.

RACHEL. No, no it is, it's lovely.

SOPHIE. I've got my booking appointment next week, and then there's all the scans…

I know it's really hard to get time off but do you think the head – ?

RACHEL. Like that mardy bum's gonna stop me.

SOPHIE. Aww!

SOPHIE goes out and brings in another two bags.

RACHEL. That you done?

SOPHIE. Yeah. Nearly.

SOPHIE brings in final two bags.

And then one more.

RACHEL. Okay, now leccy-cupboard all of it. And don't just stuff it in there…

SOPHIE heads back towards the door.

Soph! I just said…

SOPHIE. Wait, wait! Got a surprise!

Guess what I found when I was clearing out my room?

RACHEL. Two-year-old slice of pizza? Family of rats?

SOPHIE rolls her eyes and heads back into the hall.

She brings in a karaoke machine.

SOPHIE. Ta-dah!

RACHEL. What's that? Karaoke machine?

SOPHIE. I'll get the dressing-up box!

RACHEL. 'Cause that's what this room needs. More crap.

SOPHIE *drags a dressing-up box out of the leccy cupboard.*

SOPHIE. Come on, Mum, you remember!

It was like our Friday-night thing!

SOPHIE *pulls out a school tie.*

Look! The Britney Spears school tie.

SOPHIE *pulls out some super-short hot pants.*

The Rihanna hot pants!

RACHEL. Here, they're not bad them.

RACHEL *takes the hot pants and measures them against herself.*

SOPHIE *pulls out a bra, onto which canisters of squirty cream have been taped (from Katy Perry's 'California Girls' video).*

SOPHIE. Aww the Katy Perry squirty-cream bra!

There was the Lady Gaga meat dress. Probably good you chucked that out.

I thought we could do it tonight. Make a real funny TikTok.

Do you seriously not remember?

RACHEL. Drawing a blank. Sorry.

SOPHIE. Oh right. No. No worries.

SOPHIE *picks up a bag and goes to take it into the leccy cupboard.*

RACHEL *picks up the mic and starts singing Blondie's 'Heart of Glass'.*

I knew you'd remember!

SOPHIE *hurriedly riffles through the box for matching Blondie wigs.*

She throws one over to RACHEL.

They duet, singing the song together.

Oh my God, I'm not even filming this!

But as she rushes to get her phone…

RACHEL. Nah, you're alright. Should be making tracks.

SOPHIE. Aww, you're not going out, are you? I had this whole evening planned…

RACHEL. I do pole on Wednesdays.

SOPHIE. Pole? You do pole-dancing?

RACHEL. Tomorrow's kick-boxing. Trace's birthday's Friday so we're going Treehouse in Hessle. But Monday, Monday I'll be well up for shaking my hips like Shakira or bringing all the boys to the yard with my milkshake…

Ugh, don't give me the smacked-bum face. I've paid my subs for the month, Soph.

SOPHIE. S'just… my first night here.

RACHEL. Exactly. I'm getting out from under your feet.

SOPHIE. What about tea though?

RACHEL. Heron's open while eight. And then you can sort out all this crap.

RACHEL *leaves.*

SOPHIE *is alone.*

Beat. Not sure what to do with herself.

She has a half-hearted go at putting some stuff away.

Then she gets bored.

She awkwardly starts singing to the baby, stroking her bump.

SOPHIE.
Hush little baby don't you cry,
Mama's going to buy you a... a...

But then forgets the words.

So she tries talking instead.

Um...

Hi.

Hey.

Sorry.

Er...

Ugh, shit.

Sorry! I shouldn't...

God, I um... Kinda thought I'd be better at this.

This, talking to you, it should be real easy, shunt it?

And, I mean, I'm pretty great at talking to all the kids at work. Lot easier than talking to the grown-ups.

But this...

Hmm. Yeah. Kinda just feel like a bit of a twat to be...

Sorry! Is twat swearing? Sorry.

Oh my God, you must think I'm...

Er, I'm your mum –

Sorry about that. Haha.

Your mum.

And you... you are... the size of a sweet pea. Aww!
I remember from my foetal development module. Was an apple seed last week so we're moving in the right direction, haha...

I love it, you know? You, growing inside me. I feel like I can feel you. I probably can't. But I feel like I can. Feel the tingly energy of it running round my nerves.

Down my back, in my arms, 'long my fingers. Keep imagining putting you on fast-forward. Having a remote and just... watching you grow. All plump, fresh skin. Dimply cheeks and hands. Growing into little outfits with matching hats, and teeny – Converse...

Sorry. Haha.

Beat.

Um... d'ya know... I don't actually know if you can actually, you know, hear me. At all.

Can you, can you hear me?

Oh, um...

Can't remember if... I mean I don't remember covering that on my...

Sorry.

SOPHIE *googles*.

No. Can't hear sounds outside the womb till eighteen weeks.

Aware she's been talking to herself.

Twat.

Scene Four

Seven Weeks Pregnant

Time: 6.30 p.m.

SOPHIE*'s just in from work, looking through the kitchen cupboards.*

RACHEL *trips on* SOPHIE*'s crap.*

RACHEL. Argh ya bastard!

  I told you to sort this lot out!

SOPHIE. I will!

  Later.

RACHEL. No, now!

SOPHIE. Mum, what's for tea?

RACHEL. Dunno, what's in your cupboard?

SOPHIE. Aww, aren't you gonna to make us something?

  Remember when we used to get everything out the cupboard and play *Ready Steady Cook*?

  Your 'cottage pie' that was basically like Spam and crisps.

RACHEL. Reckon that would of worked if we hant only had Space Raiders.

  What was that...? That Cheesestring...

SOPHIE. Cheesestring Super Noodle Bake! I literally still make that. So good!

  Do you know what? Today I could really go for my Tuna...

  RACHEL *retches.*

RACHEL. Soph...

SOPHIE. It wasn't that bad!

RACHEL. What's the rule?

SOPHIE. I actually finished it.

RACHEL. What is the rule?

SOPHIE. We don't talk about Tuna Sweetcorn Angel Delight.

RACHEL *retches again*.

Aww that was such a cute game.

RACHEL. Wunt call it cute.

SOPHIE. What?

RACHEL. Only used to do it with you 'cause we dint have owt in.

SOPHIE. Oh. I didn't...

RACHEL. Yeah.

Beat.

SOPHIE. We don't have to do that, you could just make me –

RACHEL. Told you, Soph. No.

SOPHIE *comes into the living room and lies down on the sofa*.

SOPHIE. Aww but I've felt really crap all day though. Pretended I was 'facilitating a game of Mums and Dads' so I could lie down for ten minutes in the home corner.

And then, end of the day, guess, just guess what time she...

RACHEL. Who?

SOPHIE. Albie's mum! Guess how late she was coming for him this time?

RACHEL (*uncomfortable*). Soph...

SOPHIE. Forty-five minutes! Forty-five minutes! Her own little boy.

RACHEL. Alright, Supernanny.

SOPHIE. He doesn't know what's going on. I get the water tray out for him as a special treat, but he's crying the whole time. Asking if she's ever coming back.

She sent him in pyjamas last week, like full-on, dirty, slept-in pyjamas. Don't know why people like her have kids if they're just gonna –

RACHEL. Mams hant exactly got it easy.

SOPHIE. She's got an Audi A1.

RACHEL. Soph, tidying!

SOPHIE. Alright, God, I'm doing it!

Can you just – ?

RACHEL. No chance.

SOPHIE. Pregnant women shouldn't be carrying stuff though.

RACHEL. Oh please. I was dancing on tables in Star and Garter night my waters broke.

SOPHIE. Yeah, yeah.

RACHEL. Had a life once y'know.

Oh and er talking of crap, there's an old cot in there of yours.

Can have it.

If you don't find summat better.

SOPHIE. What you've still…? You kept it? Aww, Mum…

How come you've still got it after all these years?

RACHEL. Well, case I have another baby.

Awkward.

Cost an absolute bomb, that er, that cot did. Half a month's wage, not even joking.

Got it day after I found out I was up the duff. Was proper terrified. Like, freaking out. Thinking, what do I do? How the hell am I gonna do this properly?

So I was like, get a proper cot. Mamas & Papas. Real over-the-top.

You hated it. Put you in it and you'd scream your head off.

'Try her in a carry cot,' they said. Dint work. 'Bouncing chair so she's upright.' Nah. Only place you'd ever sleep was next to me. Every night, I was going to sleep with your hot little chicken-nugget breath on my cheek.

SOPHIE. Mum! You shouldn't do that! It increases the risk of sudden infant death syndrome.

Seriously, I had this course at work. Baby could roll off, get smothered.

RACHEL. Oh, well. You're here, aren't you? Lived to tell the tale.

SOPHIE. And it's been proved to breed dependancy as well...

RACHEL *gets up*.

Wait. Where you going?

RACHEL. For God's sake... My own bleeding bathroom, that alright?

SOPHIE. Oh, so you're actually staying in?

RACHEL. To get ready for Sesh.

SOPHIE. 'Sesh'?

RACHEL. Yeah, like at Polar Bear. Down Spring Bank. Sesh. All the local bands and –

SOPHIE. I know what it is!

RACHEL. Don't really think it's your scene. They aren't gonna be playing Taylor Swift.

SOPHIE. I don't even listen to Taylor that much any more, actually!

Just... ironically.

RACHEL. Right.

SOPHIE. I had a thing I wanted to, you know, ask you.

RACHEL. Go on then.

SOPHIE. Aw well, it's not really the sorta thing I can just, you know, say.

It's a bit...

It's sort of...

RACHEL. Soph, come on 'cause I wanna do liquid eyeliner –

SOPHIE. Liquid eyeliner?

RACHEL. Yeah, and it'll go tits-up if I'm rushing.

SOPHIE. Okay it's like… Well yeah so since I got… Since I found out about the baby. I guess…

Well it's like Helen at work. She's just got this amazing support network. Like her mum and dad have Oscar so she and Dan can do their date night. And they take him to Puddle Ducks on a Friday…

RACHEL. And if Snotty Helen jumped off the Humber Bridge…

SOPHIE. I'm just saying! It's made me think a lot about family. And where I came from.

RACHEL. Oh heck.

SOPHIE. And, building bridges…

RACHEL. Okay. Okay. Yeah. No you're… Yeah. Yeah, yeah. You're right.

SOPHIE. Yeah?

RACHEL. Yeah. I've, um, I've always kinda thought this day would come if I'm being honest.

Course you wanna know where you came from.

SOPHIE. Mum, honestly, that's such a relief.

RACHEL. But if it dunt work out how you want, you're not to get yourself upset. 'Cause it won't be no reflection on you.

SOPHIE. No. I know. But I'm sure…

RACHEL. I'll make some calls around the old Spids scene. See if anyone's got a number for him.

SOPHIE. Him?

RACHEL. Your dad.

SOPHIE. Oh, no. God, no. Why would I want to…?

RACHEL. 'Cause you said, 'bout family.

SOPHIE. I was on about Nan.

RACHEL. Nan?

SOPHIE. Like I know you and her don't really like, get on.

RACHEL. I wunt say that.

SOPHIE. It's been three and a half years.

RACHEL. Has it?

SOPHIE. Yeah, since Toby Carvery.

When you walked out holding your plate.

RACHEL. Ten-pound-nineteen that roast cost.

SOPHIE. What happened? What did she say?

RACHEL. Nothing!

SOPHIE. So you don't have a problem with her?

RACHEL. No! It's just been hard. With the lockdowns. And her living so far away.

SOPHIE. Garden Village.

RACHEL. That's two buses.

SOPHIE. Okay.

RACHEL. Okay.

SOPHIE. So I'll just go ahead then.

RACHEL. Go ahead?

SOPHIE *opens a bag-for-life and passes* RACHEL *a card from it.*

SOPHIE. Okay so I'm thinking…

She opens the card 'To a wonderful great-grandma.' And she's like 'GREAT-grandma? What is going on?'

She turns round, you jump out with this…

SOPHIE *hands* RACHEL *a confetti cannon from the bag.*

RACHEL. Confetti cannon?

SOPHIE. Then we pump up the inflatable baby…

What? Is it a bit…?

It's just to really stand out on TikTok, it's got to be…

RACHEL. Soph…

SOPHIE. I just want my baby to have a relationship with my nan. I don't get why you've got such a problem.

RACHEL. Int me with the problem.

SOPHIE. Ugh, look, it's fine. There's confetti cannons I can get with a timer so if you don't want to be involved…

RACHEL. It's not that. I just think… It's not the best idea.

SOPHIE. Alright, well if you can think of something better…

Just, I've spent twelve-pound-fifty in Home Bargains.

RACHEL. Oh right, so you're always scranning my milk but you've got enough to waste twelve-pound-fifty on tat?

SOPHIE. Mum!

RACHEL. I just don't think it's gonna go down how you want.

She… When I told her, your nan, when I said I was having you…

She loves you now. Obviously.

But she… blew her top.

SOPHIE. Whereas you handled it amazingly.

RACHEL. Why don't…?

SOPHIE. What?

What were you going to say?

RACHEL. Why don't I maybe call her?

SOPHIE. Really?

RACHEL. Yeah.

SOPHIE. Will you actually though?

RACHEL. Yes!

SOPHIE. How do I know…?

RACHEL. I will, alright?

Long as you promise me, swear down, you won't say owt to her about this baby.

SOPHIE. Yeah, whatever. Oh my God, Mum, thank you. You are the best!

SOPHIE *hugs* RACHEL.

RACHEL *heads towards the bathroom to get ready.*

RACHEL (*under her breath*). Yeah. I'll talk to her.

Later.

Scene Five

Seven Weeks Pregnant

Time: 6.30 p.m.

RACHEL *lies on the sofa, with a bag of frozen peas held to her jaw.*

SOPHIE. Mum? What've you done?

Why's everything in the fridge got 'Rachel' wrote on it?

RACHEL. 'How are you, Mum? How was your day?' Well, Sophie, today, we had the head doing a learning walk 'cause they're looking at laying off, sorry, 'restructuring' TAs.

And my precious one-to-one suddenly decides he's gonna lob a chair through the interactive whiteboard. Fortunately for the school budget, chair misses the whiteboard. And smacks muggins here right in the gob.

SOPHIE. Oh, yeah, God, poor you that's, really shit… What about the food though?

RACHEL. Oh, see, I was just… helping you out.

SOPHIE. What?

RACHEL. Well, you just seem to be getting a bit muddled recently. Pregnancy brain and all that...

SOPHIE. 'Muddled'?

RACHEL. Helping yourself to the odd tin of sweetcorn. My Aldi fake Special K. I've said nowt.

But then today I find out you've crossed a line.

SOPHIE. What?

RACHEL. And ate MY Slimming World sausages –

SOPHIE. Oh.

RACHEL. What cost me THREE-POUND-SEVENTY-FIVE –

SOPHIE. I didn't know it was such a big –

RACHEL. THREE-POUND-SEVENTY-FIVE.

AND they only do them in Big Heron.

SOPHIE. Well, sorry.

It's just Helen was saying in our diet and nutrition training how she ate loads of protein with her Oscar. And he came out ten pounds and she was straight back in her jeans, minute he was born. So I got a load of chickpeas and lentils and made this tagine thingy. Enough for a whole week.

But it was all claggy, like eating Play-Doh! I chucked my guts up for a full-on hour. And then I saw them sausages...

RACHEL. That stuck-up cow might have money to chuck down the lav. But I hant!

Look, I treat myself very, very rarely. And them sausages were what kept me going through a properly shitty day. And I come home, can practically hear them sizzling in the Frylight cooking spray. I open the fridge and what do I see?

What do I see, Soph?

SOPHIE. Alright.

RACHEL. THEY WERE SYN-FREE.

SOPHIE. Fine. I didn't realise you were gonna –

RACHEL. I have spent months shopping around, Soph. Figuring out my system. Heron, Iceland, Aldi mark-downs at seven-thirty. Keeping my big shop under twenty quid a week. I aren't having your fat arse –

SOPHIE. 'Fat arse'?

RACHEL. I aren't having your beautiful… fat arse coming in here and wrecking it now.

SOPHIE. Oh right, I'll just starve then, shall I?

RACHEL. What?

SOPHIE. Oh, yeah, you'd love that. If I just… faded away.

RACHEL. Oh here we go –

SOPHIE. Wouldn't have to put up with me then, would you?

RACHEL. Roll up, ladies and gentlemen –

SOPHIE. Well you know what, I'm sorry alright?

RACHEL. Get your tickets here.

SOPHIE. Sorry for… existing.

RACHEL. There's about to be a bloody performance.

SOPHIE. Me? Me, performance?

I'm just saying right, I live here too you know.

RACHEL. Oh yeah, I KNOW.

SOPHIE. Mum!

Beat.

RACHEL *takes a deep breath.*

RACHEL. Look, bottom line is you're earning, right?

SOPHIE. Well yeah, obviously.

RACHEL. Great. Then you can forget Snotty Helen and her Snuggle Pods and her tagines. And buy your own bloody sausages.

So, from now on, every –

SOPHIE. Do you realise how crazy you sound?

RACHEL. Listen to me, every time you see food what says 'Rachel' on it, I want you to back off. Alright?

And when you see a piece of 'quinoa' bollocks with 'Sophie' wrote on, knock yourself out.

RACHEL *storms out.*

SOPHIE *watches her go and gets out her phone.*

SOPHIE. Right.

SOPHIE *starts texting.*

Scene Six

Eleven Weeks Pregnant

Time: 6.45 a.m.

RACHEL *is in the living room, ready for work.*

She's about to bite into a slice of toast when…

Vomit sounds. From SOPHIE *in the bathroom.*

RACHEL (*under her breath*). Oh for God's… Here we go.

(*To* SOPHIE.) Make sure you give it a good flush, love. I've still got my teeth to do.

And bleach the seat after.

SOPHIE *emerges. Looking like shit.*

You alright, love?

SOPHIE. Oh yeah. It's just my morning routine. Get up. Vomit. Shower. Vomit. Brush hair. Bit of concealer, try to get the under-eye bags covered before the next vomit.

Sit on the sofa and cry. Vomit. Get bus to work. Get off halfway through to vomit. Get on next bus ten minutes later. Get to work. Vomit.

Sort the kids' Weetabix. Vomit.

Been pretending to Helen I've been having dodgy curries. She keeps saying she's going to write an 'exposé' 'bout local takeaways in *Hull Daily Mail*.

RACHEL. Oh, love. Sit yourself down…

SOPHIE. I better get to work.

SOPHIE suddenly thinks she's gonna faint.

RACHEL leaps up.

RACHEL. I've got you.

You really think you're up to going in?

SOPHIE. Yeah. Yeah. I've got my…

She produces a kid's plastic bucket.

My bucket. 'Cause carrier bags've got them little holes.

I just need to get through it. 'Cause, you know, pregnancy isn't an illness. I can't let it stop me from…

And I'm fit, healthy. Young. Statistically I'm the optimum age biologically so…

So…

So…

SOPHIE voms into the bucket.

RACHEL strokes her hair – and tries not to look grossed out.

RACHEL. Look, love, why not have a day off, yeah?

SOPHIE. No!

RACHEL. Just… listen to your body.

Seriously, Soph, past week you've been going round looking like a bin of gone-off rice pudding.

SOPHIE. Thanks, Mum.

RACHEL. Only has to be a day, dunt it? Put your feet up, bit of *Homes Under the Hammer.* And go in looking semi-human on Wednesday. Yeah?

'Cause you gotta look after the baby, hant you? It int just all about you.

SOPHIE. I can't… I haven't had a day off sick in six years.

RACHEL. Come on, get your head outta Snotty Helen's arse. The place won't actually combust without you for twenty-four hours.

SOPHIE. Honestly, I can't –

RACHEL wraps SOPHIE into a hug.

RACHEL. Want this bloody tough in Year 10, was you? Twagging double-science Mondays, PE Wednesdays, Friday swimming…

SOPHIE. If I don't go in I don't get paid.

RACHEL. I know, love, I'm just worried –

SOPHIE. I'm not throwing away sixty-five-pound-sixty.

RACHEL. I get it. But I don't think you've got a choice.

SOPHIE. Mum, stop it, alright? I've got my bucket. I'm going in.

SOPHIE leaves for work.

RACHEL heads to the bathroom.

It stinks.

RACHEL. For God's…

She puts her face up her jumper and grabs some Dettol Spray before going into the bathroom.

Scene Seven

Still Eleven Weeks Pregnant

Time: 5.30 p.m.

LINDA *is standing in the middle of the room. She's on crutches and her leg is in a pot.*

SOPHIE *walks in from the bathroom.*

And screams.

SOPHIE. Oh my God oh my God! Get out! Being serious, get out! Now!

SOPHIE *picks up a trainer to defend herself.*

LINDA. Sophie, darling!

SOPHIE. Nan?

LINDA. Oh! Frightened the living daylights out of me.

SOPHIE *drops the trainer.*

SOPHIE. Sorry! Really, sorry!

How did you… [get in]?

LINDA. I'm sorry, intruding on you like this. Just I thought, you know, they're family, they won't mind.

And the keys were in the door.

SOPHIE. Again? Ugh!

I've just been really… tired recently.

LINDA. And then I come in and see you've been burgled…

SOPHIE. What?

SOPHIE *looks anxiously around the room. Realises* LINDA *means the mess.*

Oh. Sorry. I was going to tidy up a bit.

SOPHIE *hastily begins tidying up.*

LINDA. Now, don't put yourself to any bother.

She's always been the same, your mam. Expecting the rest of us to go picking up after her.

Oof, sorry. Getting a little cramp in this leg.

SOPHIE. Here, let me...

SOPHIE *helps* LINDA *to the sofa.*

What happened to your leg?

LINDA. Fuss over nothing.

She's not here is she? Your mam?

SOPHIE. Oh, no. She must be late back from work.

I'm supposed to be. Got sent home. Had a bit of a... dodgy tummy. Then one of the kids nicked my sick bucket and the only thing close enough was the sandpit.

LINDA. You poor love!

LINDA *clearly doesn't want to catch anything.*

I can make it from here.

SOPHIE. Yeah, it's been really tough.

Can I get you anything? Tea or...?

LINDA. Oh, no. Don't want to put you out if you're not well. Just, is my bag still out there?

She gestures to the hallway.

SOPHIE. Bag? Oh yeah...

SOPHIE *hurries out and returns with a travel bag, a carrier bag and a commode.*

LINDA. Aren't you a love? And the split of Nana Joan!

SOPHIE. Really?

LINDA. It's all round the eyes.

Did you say there was tea on offer?

SOPHIE. Oh, yes.

LINDA. Just if you're making.

SOPHIE *heads into the kitchen and starts looking in cupboards.*

SOPHIE. Really, really sorry. I actually don't have any tea with Sophie wrote on. Unless I use Mum's bag from this morning, give it a good squeeze.

Just… been off work a couple of days this week, so haven't been able to get to the shops.

LINDA. Hot water'll be fine, love.

With just a little drop of cold. And lemon and a bit of honey, if you have it.

There's nobody… out there is there?

SOPHIE *checks out the window.*

SOPHIE. Um, no? Who would be…?

LINDA. That patient-transporter service. From the hospital. Take my hat off to the NHS, I really do. But that lot… Incompetent. Talking all this nonsense about packing me off to a respite home. Ridiculous. I mean, do I look like I belong in a home to you? Says to them, should check my Fitbit. Ten thousand steps a day!

SOPHIE. Because of the leg? Looks really nasty. What happened?

LINDA. Honestly, Sophie, love. You don't need to worry about me. Little accident at work.

This lass, barely out of primary school, they had her 'assisting' me on chilled produce. I've had more assistance from an athlete's foot.

SOPHIE *returns with a mug of hot water.*

SOPHIE. Sorry, chilled…? I thought you were a bra-fitter.

LINDA. Oh gosh no. Not since Marks in town shut down. I've had to diversify. 'Operations for a chilled and frozen food warehouse.'

Anyway, Imogen… Probably TikTok-ing or Twit-Twating. She drops a Yeo Valley Yogurt on the floor. No thought for the spillage procedure. I come over with a crate of chicken avocado sandwiches. End up spreadeagled across the aisle.

SOPHIE. Oh God! Poor you, having a fall –

LINDA. I didn't 'have a fall'! I'm not ninety years old. I had an accident at work! If this was the nineties I'd be entitled to compensation.

SOPHIE. Sorry.

LINDA. So there I am. Twenty hours in A&E with all the drunks and screaming babies.

Poor dear next to me coughing up a lung. All the while knowing Imogen's going to be merrily stacking everything willy-nilly and half my produce is going to go off.

SOPHIE. So they're not sending you to a home?

LINDA. I wouldn't hear of it. I said to them, even if I had eight hundred and forty pound a week I certainly wouldn't be spending it watching *Bargain Hunt* with people old enough to be my parents.

SOPHIE. So…

SOPHIE *looks at all* LINDA*'s bags.*

Where do you think you'll go?

LINDA. Well Gillian from work is out because she's doing Airbnb in her box room and I tried Mandy, you remember Mardy Mandy at number 5A? But her Scott's just moved his new woman in. Turned Mandy's dining room into a love nest apparently.

SOPHIE. Yeah, God, that's really tough.

LINDA. Oh, no, don't worry about me.

I want to hear about you! Read your lovely message in hospital –

SOPHIE. Oh you got that? It's just I wasn't sure when you left me on read.

LINDA. No, I was delighted! You said you was back at your mam's and I thought, first chance I get, I'll go and visit my gorgeous granddaughter.

SOPHIE. Really? That's... So Mum doesn't know you're here?

LINDA. I haven't heard hide nor hair of your mam since she walked out of Toby Carvery –

SOPHIE. Holding her plate. I remember.

LINDA. Oh Sophie, the look on that lovely waitress's face. I've never been so mortified.

SOPHIE. She did um, take it back. The plate.

Look, Nan, if you're really struggling, maybe...?

LINDA. Really? Oh Sophie, I can't tell you! That would be such a weight off.

SOPHIE. But I need to ask Mum...

LINDA. I know what she's like but I looked after Nana Joan for three years. Surely she can put up with me till this daft pot comes off? You won't even know I'm here.

SOPHIE. I'm not sure.

LINDA. And all this, in a way, it's a blessing in disguise. Means I get to spend a bit of time with my Sophie!

SOPHIE. Yeah?

LINDA. Because God knows, I've missed out on so much, haven't I?

SOPHIE. Yeah! Yeah, I feel the same. All the important... life events.

LINDA. Exactly.

SOPHIE. Which was... kinda why I messaged you, actually. I um... Well I've had some news.

LINDA. Is that right? I think I know, you know.

SOPHIE. Really?

LINDA. Mm. Got that air about you.

SOPHIE. Oh wow, because I did think actually...

LINDA. Aww, Sophie, I'm ever so proud!

SOPHIE. Yeah?

LINDA. You are, aren't you? First in our family to get into university!

Oh, you're going to have the best time, walking into lectures in one of them floaty scarves. Folder in one hand, one of them reusable coffee cups in the other. Reading out on the grass with your pals...

Wait till I tell Mardy Mandy.

And Imogen! She always tries to make out her NVQ is equivalent but...

SOPHIE. Er, no. That's not... I mean I still want to do that... There's this learning support degree... But not at the moment...

LINDA. Oh.

SOPHIE. I'm really sorry, Nan, but I'm...

SOPHIE *takes a deep breath*.

LINDA. What? Not up in court?

SOPHIE. Pregnant.

LINDA. Pregnant?

SOPHIE. Yeah.

Beat.

That's why I'm back at Mum's.

Just till I can get my own place.

I would of told you before but... Mum said best not.

LINDA. She did, did she?

SOPHIE. Well I think it was just that when she said she was having me, you found it a bit... hard.

LINDA. No, no. That was different.

You've got your head screwed on. Good job?

SOPHIE. Nursery nurse. Up to thirty, thirty-five hours most weeks now. Normally, when I'm up to it.

LINDA. Whereas your mam, seven jobs in –

SOPHIE. Six months, yeah!

LINDA. And you'll be prepared.

SOPHIE. Got a spreadsheet and everything.

LINDA. And you'll have a nice fella to rub your back in the labour room.

SOPHIE. Oh, er, not... No.

LINDA. Ah well, can't have everything. Mine went and got knocked off his bike before Rachel was one.

'Ride careful.' I said. 'I'm always careful.' Last thing he says to me.

Beat.

SOPHIE. So, you're not mad at me?

LINDA. Mad at you? Sophie, I'm made up for you! My first grandchild!

SOPHIE. Great-grandchild.

LINDA. Exactly!

Oh and you were such a bonny baby, Sophie! Lovely round cheeks and this big mop of hair.

LINDA *starts welling up.*

Oh, what am I like? I'm going, I'm going.

SOPHIE. Wait! Um, do you think we could do it again?

LINDA. Again?

SOPHIE. My reveal? For TikTok? It's just I've got these confetti cannons…

LINDA. Do you know, I would absolutely love that. But first, I think I'm going to clear myself a little corner and get some shut-eye.

SOPHIE. Oh, right. Yeah. I can take the floor if –

LINDA. Sophie! I wouldn't dream of it! You're a pregnant women.

Now, I couldn't trouble you…

She holds out her arm for SOPHIE *to help her up.*

SOPHIE. Of course…

SOPHIE *helps* LINDA *up and passes her her crutches.*

LINDA *takes them and starts slowly making her way towards the bedroom.*

LINDA. I'll be absolutely fine in your mother's bed.

SOPHIE *is left alone.*

SOPHIE. Shit.

Scene Eight

Eleven Weeks Pregnant

Time: 4.30 a.m.

RACHEL *sneaks in from a night out – drunk, and wearing a bodycon dress of* SOPHIE*'s.*

SOPHIE*'s been asleep on the sofa.*

SOPHIE. Mum, ssssh! What are you doing?

Have you only just got in?

RACHEL. Um...

SOPHIE. Mum, it's... oh my God, it's half-four. Have you seriously only just got in?

RACHEL. Maybe...

You tidied up in here?

SOPHIE. Keep your voice down! Where've you been?

RACHEL. Er...

SOPHIE. Don't give me that. Where the hell you been till half-past four? God's sake – it's a school night.

RACHEL. Mm. Can't tell ya.

SOPHIE. Why?

RACHEL. 'Cause. You're just gonna be all, you know, about it.

SOPHIE. Ssssh! I'm never all...

SOPHIE *sees the dress.*

Oh my God is that my dress?

RACHEL. Well, int like you're going to be fitting into it for a while, is it?

SOPHIE. You can't just go around taking my things!

RACHEL. I had a date.

SOPHIE. A date?

RACHEL. Yeah.

SOPHIE. But… you don't go on dates…

   Since when? Since when d'you go on dates?

RACHEL. Since… I dunno.

SOPHIE. Well, who was he?

RACHEL. I dunno.

SOPHIE. You 'dunno'?

RACHEL. Some bloke off Plenty of Fish.

SOPHIE. Ugh.

RACHEL. Don't worry, I aren't gonna be making him your new
   daddy. Aw, Soph, he was so cringe. One point he was tryna be
   all like, 'Are you winter? 'Cause you'll be cumming soon.'
   I mean, mate it's bloody June, how long d'ya think I take?

SOPHIE. Well he sounds –

RACHEL. Bless him. He was only twenty-two.

SOPHIE. Twenty-two! Ugh, Mum!

RACHEL. And don't you worry. I used properly fitting
   protection –

SOPHIE. Sssshh!!

RACHEL. What? I've got needs too, y'know.

SOPHIE. Shush. Really. Please.

RACHEL. I wanna actually be held once in a while. Have my
   ear bitten. That fanny flutter you get when someone actually
   wants your body. Int just Gen Z that, you know.

   You lot need reminding, us has-beens aren't fucking invisible.

SOPHIE. Oh my… Please can you stop? Why would I wanna
   hear that? About my own… Ugh, why would I…?

RACHEL. Ugh, knew you was gonna… You bloody asked.
   Sticking your neb in my business. Int my fault if you get
   upset –

SOPHIE. No! All this... This isn't you! You're all playing silly
    games and library trips and farm parks and remembering my
    cooking ingredients.

RACHEL. Look, you've been moved out four years. I've
    matured.

SOPHIE. Matured?

    For God's sake, you're about to be a nana. It's embarrassing.

RACHEL. Embarrassing? Oh, I'm embarrassing you, am I?

    Well, know what, Soph? I don't actually give a shit. 'Cause
    I need this. Getting a few bevs in on a weekend. Pole class.
    Having actual sex.

    I need this. I really, really need this.

    Beat.

    I'm off to bed... What the fuck??

    LINDA *is standing in the doorway on crutches, in PJs.*

LINDA. Language, Rachel!

RACHEL. Is she... real?

LINDA. Goodness that's a lot of make-up.

RACHEL. How long've you been...?

LINDA. Long enough. Unfortunately.

    RACHEL *whirls round to* SOPHIE.

RACHEL. I told you not to call her.

SOPHIE. You promised me you were going to call her!

LINDA. Now, nothing good ever happens after two a.m., as
    Nana Joan used to say. So let's all get some sleep. Rachel,
    get that stuff off your face and come to bed.

RACHEL. You're not stopping here.

SOPHIE. Mum, her leg.

LINDA. I'm sorry, Sophie, this was so stupid of me, to think my own daughter might let me stay a few days when I'm laid up. I should have known.

RACHEL. Stay where? We hant got the room.

LINDA. Your mam's right, it was a daft idea. If you can just help me to the door with my crutches and that commode, Sophie, I won't trouble you any more...

But it would have been so lovely, Sophie, spending time with you, especially in your condition.

RACHEL. Soph, I told you not to say owt to her about this baby.

SOPHIE. Yeah well she was really happy about it, weren't you, Nan?

LINDA. Of course! Over the moon!

RACHEL. She's just trying to show me up!

LINDA. You don't need me for that.

RACHEL. I'll call you a taxi.

SOPHIE. It's four in the morning!

RACHEL. I don't care.

SOPHIE. Mum!

RACHEL. She int gonna be free childcare when the baby comes, if that's what you're thinking.

SOPHIE. No, I wasn't!

Honestly, Nan! I mean, only if you wanted to...

LINDA. Of course! It'll be nice. After all I've missed out on.

SOPHIE. Thank you!

RACHEL. That's bollocks and you know it.

LINDA. Well it has, I don't like to complain, but it's been hard for me, Rachel. These last few years. Going through the lockdowns on my own.

RACHEL. Dint see you picking up the phone.

LINDA. I didn't like to be a bother.

SOPHIE. She means after Toby Carvery.

RACHEL. Yes thank you, Sophie.

LINDA. And I'm sorry if I upset you, Rachel. But those times were painful to all of us, I felt Sophie had a right to know.

RACHEL. Out. Now.

SOPHIE *blocks the door.*

SOPHIE. Nan, don't listen to her.

Mum, you're overreacting.

RACHEL. Soph, you have no idea. Way she treated me when I was having you. 'Worst thing what ever happened to her. You're too full of yourself to bring up a kid.'

LINDA. Rachel! I was worried. One minute you were this quiet, clever girl.

SOPHIE. Really? Mum?

LINDA. So much potential. Could of been a lawyer, accountant. And then she gets in with this wrong crowd. Those... moths.

RACHEL. Goths!

LINDA. And suddenly it's all boys and booze and funny cigarettes! One day she comes home, tells me that she's pregnant and I... I just knew you weren't ready for motherhood. And, well, I'm afraid I was proved right.

SOPHIE. Oh no, Nan, Mum's... Well, when I was growing up she was, really, really great.

LINDA. When she bothered to turn up.

RACHEL. Mam!

SOPHIE. No, she was always like really there for me.

LINDA. Not always, dear.

SOPHIE. What?

LINDA. Have you still not told her this?

SOPHIE. What? What is it?

RACHEL. Mam, for God's sakes. It's nothing.

LINDA. I wouldn't call it nothing, Rachel.

SOPHIE. What?

RACHEL. Don't listen to her, Soph.

LINDA. How old was she? Three months?

    And you just up and –

SOPHIE. What's she talking about, Mum?

RACHEL. Sophie, it's… You've gotta understand… When you was born, I went from this proper fun teenager. Out six nights a week, loads of mates, to losing it all. No one ever came round to see me.

    And there was this one time, Shel's birthday. Mam said she'd have you.

LINDA. Well I didn't exactly get much of a choice.

RACHEL. Old Zoological, it was s'posed to be. Then round Bev Road. Just like old times. Bought this silver dress from British Heart Foundation specially.

    But before we've even ordered, she's ringing the pub. Saying you've been screaming since second I left. Half-hour later, food's just arrived. Barman comes over, Mam's on the phone again. All the girls are like, 'She's fine, she's just crying, leave her.' But I can feel the milk starting to leak through my dress…

    I got the first bus back. End up sat on the bed, eight p.m., in my soggy silver dress, holding you and crying and crying. Both of us fucking crying.

    Silence.

SOPHIE. Well, sorry I ruined your social life.

RACHEL. That's not what I meant!

LINDA. Tell her what happened the next morning.

RACHEL. Please. Don't.

LINDA (*to* SOPHIE). You were just crying and crying.

RACHEL. You've got to understand. I want well. Dint know who I was any more.

LINDA. So I go into you and...

RACHEL. Mam.

LINDA. There you were in that great big cot of yours. All alone. Soaked through.

Silence.

SOPHIE. No... 'Cause... Didn't we, Mum? Tell her! We slept in the same bed, every night.

LINDA. She left you, with me. And she didn't come back for six weeks.

SOPHIE. Mum? That's just not true. You wouldn't. Mum!

ACT TWO

Scene One

Twelve Weeks Pregnant

Time: 4 p.m.

SOPHIE *stands alone, in the Blondie wig, singing 'Heart of Glass' sadly into the karaoke machine. She sings the first two verses of the song.*

She's got her phone on a tripod.

LINDA *walks in.*

SOPHIE. Sorry!

I was just… For TikTok.

Me and Mum used to play this stupid game. Back when she was nice. This is, was our favourite. But honestly I can… [stop.]

But LINDA *picks up the other mic and starts singing along.*

SOPHIE*'s startled but goes with it. They finish the song together.*

As the music fades out…

LINDA*'s leg buckles under her. She struggles to the sofa.*

SOPHIE *goes to help her. But she shakes her off.*

Nan?

LINDA. Takes me right back, that song.

SOPHIE. Are you okay?

LINDA (*ignoring her*). Lower-sixth party, 1979, Romeo and Juliet's. Me and my pal Sharon Phillips, dancing round our handbags after one too many Cinzano and lemonades!

SOPHIE. Didn't know you did sixth form.

LINDA (*proud*). Oh yes. Newland High. Only twelve of us that stayed on. 'History, geography and general studies.'

Didn't last long. Met my Dave in The Old English Gentleman and I knew before he said hello he was the one for me.

Nana Joan said 'Don't want to keep a good man like that waiting.' So that was that. I let him sweep me off my feet and into Marks. Fell for our Rachel not long after.

Sharon stuck with it though. Saw her the other day at Hull Royal. Charge nurse no less. Which, I mean, is wonderful for her because when we were in school she thought Switzerland was in Lincolnshire.

All in the past now.

SOPHIE. Nan, can I ask you something?

LINDA. Of course, darling.

SOPHIE. What are you doing tomorrow?

LINDA. Same as every day. *Can't Pay? We'll Take It Away!*, *Judge Judy*, *Judge Rinder*... I'm practically qualified for the bar at this point. Endless adverts about stairlifts and incontinence pads...

Or of course I could read some of the so-called 'literature' Mardy Mandy dropped round, full of girls riding bareback and men with 'throbbing members'.

SOPHIE. It's my scan.

LINDA. Of course it is!

SOPHIE. My first scan.

LINDA. So exciting.

SOPHIE. And I'd really like you to come with me.

LINDA. Oh.

What about your mam, love?

SOPHIE. Kinda be a bit awkward considering we're not speaking.

LINDA. I really wouldn't want to start anything. She is letting me stay here.

And sharing a bed with me is no picnic at the moment. This leg, honestly, mind of its own. Jumps for England.

SOPHIE. She won't care.

This whole 'Nana' thing. It's not exactly good for her image.

LINDA. I really don't want to get in the way.

SOPHIE. Okay. It's… I'll go on my own.

LINDA. Don't say that.

SOPHIE. Just, I guess I kind of thought… Well, when Mum left, you were there for me, weren't you?

LINDA. Well…

SOPHIE. I just wanted to invite you to say thank you.

Please.

LINDA. I… Yes. Yes, I'd be delighted.

SOPHIE. You'll come? Really?

LINDA. Really.

They hug.

Now, what's next? Have you got any ABBA?

Scene Two

Twelve Weeks Pregnant

Time: 1.20 p.m.

LINDA *and* SOPHIE *are looking at a scan photo.*

LINDA. Takes your breath away, doesn't it?

SOPHIE. I didn't realise they cost five pound.

LINDA. Never forget my first one with our Rachel. The size of that nose. I just had to pray she'd grow into it.

But this little one, perfect proportions!

SOPHIE. Well...

LINDA. Oh no, I wouldn't worry about all that, what was it they said? About it being...

SOPHIE. Small for the dates.

LINDA. We tend to be fine-boned on my side of the family.

Rachel always took after her dad.

Oh and um... Figs and prunes'll help. For your problem. Down below.

SOPHIE. Thanks.

LINDA. You thought about names yet?

SOPHIE. Sort of. A bit. I've got a shortlist of thirty-eight.

LINDA. 'Anthea.'

SOPHIE. What?

LINDA. If it's a girl. 'Anthea.'

Always liked it. My parents wanted to call it me. But when I come out they said I looked more like a 'Linda'.

SOPHIE. Oh.

LINDA. You have to wonder what sort of life I could of had as an Anthea.

Beat. LINDA*'s lost in thought.*

SOPHIE. Thanks. I'll um… think about it.

LINDA. Do.

SOPHIE. And thanks so much as well, you know, for coming with me.

LINDA. Pleasure.

SOPHIE. No, it really means a lot. You being here.

LINDA. Always.

SOPHIE. Anyway, sorry, I'd better…

LINDA. Oh you're in this afternoon?

SOPHIE. Sort of.

LINDA. Oh, lucky you. Never thought I'd miss clocking in at six every day.

SOPHIE. I'm not actually in. Well, um, not really. It's silly. I just wanted to… Well my boss, Helen. She's kind of more of a 'work mum' really, haha. Now I can tell people, I just wanted her to be the first to… Gonna give her like a present bag and then in it's gonna be this little baby vest – 'Best Oops Ever.' Finally get to use that confetti cannon… It's silly.

LINDA. Not at all! It's lovely you and her are so close.

SOPHIE. Yeah. Yeah it is.

LINDA. And you'll be so lucky, being able to bring baby into work with you…

SOPHIE. I can't actually afford Helen's rates.

LINDA. Oh?

SOPHIE. Just at the moment. Maybe, you know, in the future, 'cause Helen says next time a level-two position comes up it's mine.

LINDA. Course it is. She's not going to want to do without you, Sophie.

SOPHIE. But I was thinking, we should do a Google Calendar.

LINDA. A what?

SOPHIE. Like an itinerary. For when the baby's here.
Synchronise our shifts.

    Just... because you said you wanted to help out... with the
    childcare.

LINDA. Oh, no. I did. Didn't I?

SOPHIE. But you don't have to if... Honestly, because it's a lot.

LINDA. No, of course.

SOPHIE. Aww phew! Thank you. That's such a relief! Don't
know how I'd go back to work if you didn't... You're gonna
have so much fun. Wriggle and giggle classes. Puddle
Ducks. Baby sensory. Baby yoga...

LINDA. Really? Oh...

    RACHEL *bursts in*.

RACHEL (*to* SOPHIE). Soph! I'm proper sorry! My one-to-one
brought his Gaboon viper into school and I had to kettle it in
a maths classroom while we waited for the RSPCA.

    But we can call them, hospital. Ask 'em to fit us in. Want me
    to call, explain?

SOPHIE. It's fine.

RACHEL. And if the hospital hant got no slots I'll play merry
hell with the school, make 'em give me the day off tomorrow.

LINDA. Think I'll um... go for a lie-down.

    Awkward silence.

RACHEL. I really am proper sorry.

SOPHIE. Told you, it's fine. I actually... already went for the
scan.

    SOPHIE *hands* RACHEL *the photo*.

    So you can just go back to work or whatever.

RACHEL. Oh God. Oh, love, I'm so sorry. Going into summat
like that on your own.

SOPHIE. I wasn't on my own.

RACHEL. What if summat had of gone wrong? And then you
    was just there –

SOPHIE. I wasn't on my own. Nan came with me.

RACHEL. Course she did. Any excuse to show me up.

SOPHIE. You know what? She was um, she was great, actually.
    Really there for me.

    And she knew all the right questions, you know, to ask. Like
    about the sickness. Hyperemesis they're calling it. With her
    having it and all.

RACHEL. So did I.

SOPHIE. And about preventing dehydration. 'Cause apparently
    that's what's causing the… you know… problems.

RACHEL. Like she's got a right to go round obsessing 'bout
    your constipation. Your bowels are my area – I'm your mam.

SOPHIE. And yeah just like how long it's gonna last. 'Cause, the
    thing with hyperemesis, it's not like normal morning sickness.
    Some cases can go on right up till the birth, you know –

RACHEL. I know! Forty weeks sucking on ice cubes. And look
    at the thanks I get.

SOPHIE. Look. Sorry. Didn't think you'd really want to come
    anyway.

RACHEL. 'Wunt wanna come'? You seriously… 'Wunt wanna
    come'?

SOPHIE. I thought you'd have better things to do.

    Beat.

RACHEL. So everything was, alright?

SOPHIE. Yeah.

    Beat.

    Bit small for the dates, they said.

RACHEL. Oh…

SOPHIE. But you know, developing how they'd expect, no sign of problems, that was all... Was all great...

RACHEL. Well, that's good, int it?

SOPHIE. Yeah.

SOPHIE *hovers*.

Beat.

Mum...

I kinda um...

I kinda...

I don't wanna sound...

You know, Mum. I don't wanna sound like I'm. I dunno. Ungrateful. Or some kinda...

Like obviously I was really, you know, happy. And relieved and everything. That baby was healthy. I mean God, I've had so many three-in-the-morning worry zones. Every night since I found out really. Where I go to one of the scans and they tell me. I dunno. There's no... heartbeat. Something like that.

But um... so yeah, I was really happy.

I came out really happy but...

And I guess I was expecting this... you know Big Moment. Where I'd see the baby and I'd be crying. Like, electricity. The sorta Moment you could play a Coldplay song underneath.

But yeah, it was just really, like a hospital appointment. I had to drink two pints of water a hour before. Whole thing was twenty minutes late so by the time they put the gel on my belly, I just kept thinking about needing a wee. We saw the baby, heard the heartbeat, they did all the checks they needed to do, quick as they could, then we saw a midwife, um... Can't remember her name. She asked her questions. We asked ours. And we left.

Is that... Did you...? Does that make me a bad mum?

RACHEL. Er, I'm sure...

SOPHIE. You don't think there's something wrong with me, do you?

RACHEL. Wrong with you?

SOPHIE. Like I'm getting… depressed. Like you.

RACHEL *hesitates. Thinks about saying something supportive. Can't.*

RACHEL. I don't know. Why don't you ask your nan?

SOPHIE *storms out of the flat.*

Time-lapse.

Twelve to Twenty-Five Weeks Pregnant

RACHEL *practising her pole moves on the doorframe and* SOPHIE *catching her.* RACHEL *stopping, embarrassed.*

***

LINDA *surreptitiously bringing a box into the living room. Looking around her, then dragging in another.*

***

LINDA *and* RACHEL *watching TV – from opposite ends of the room.*

***

SOPHIE *sneaking in, taking food from the kitchen, peeling off a label marked 'Rachel' and eating it.*

***

LINDA *struggling to get up on her own. Getting angry, frustrated, then emotional.*

***

SOPHIE *feeling the baby kick for the first time.*

***

RACHEL *finding an 'It's a Girl' balloon. Alone.*

Scene Three

Twenty-Five Weeks Pregnant

Time: 4.20 p.m

SOPHIE*'s now visibly pregnant, wearing a 'Mum-to-Be' sash and dragging a Deluxe Snuggle Pod with a pink bow on it. And her bucket.*

She enters like a ninja.

Looks round.

SOPHIE. Mum?

Mum?

No sign.

She edges towards the kitchen…

Still watching her back.

Carefully, so carefully takes a loaf of bread – discarding the label marked 'Rachel'.

Takes a bite…

RACHEL *leaps out from behind the sofa.*

RACHEL. Fucking knew it!

SOPHIE. Ahh!!

RACHEL. Come in here and hand it over.

Sophie.

Hand it over.

SOPHIE. But I… haven't really eaten much. Today. At all.

Helen got this sushi platter for the baby shower 'cause she's on the five:two diet. But I'm not allowed raw fish and it really stunk so I kept having to go off and use my bucket.

And by the time I felt better, I went into the kitchen for the leftover cheese straws but she'd bagged them all up for Manon –

RACHEL. Manon? What?

SOPHIE. Her French Bulldog. Oh and they um, they all clubbed together and got me this, Deluxe Snuggle Pod for beside the bed and yeah I should be real grateful but –

RACHEL. I don't wanna hear it, Soph. If you're hungry get your arse down Aldi.

SOPHIE. Ugh, fine, have your fucking bread.

She screws up the bread.

RACHEL. Sophie! Sophie, stop it! Don't screw it up! Sophie, that's good Hovis!

SOPHIE. God, I'm such a...

I'm such a fucking...

RACHEL. Sophie. Calm down.

It's just your hormones –

SOPHIE. It's not... my... fucking... hormones...

It's...

Ugh, dunt matter. Not like you'd care.

RACHEL. Soph.

SOPHIE. Helen hant put me on the rota next week. At all.

RACHEL. Fucking hell.

SOPHIE. And, and well to be honest, it's not the first time.

RACHEL. What do you mean?

SOPHIE (*Helen's posh voice*). 'Funding's tight. Happening everywhere. All making sacrifices. Sharing out the hours.'

RACHEL. Well how much's she put Toni in for?

SOPHIE. Thirty-five.

RACHEL. Bullshit!

SOPHIE. My maternity pay's going to be right down now. Ninety per cent of my average earnings. That's bugger-all at the moment!

That's if she has me back at all.

It's 'cause of the sickness. Hyperemesis. I know it is.

RACHEL. Nah. How would Snotty Helen know about...?

SOPHIE....

RACHEL. Oh Soph, you dint?

SOPHIE. Just um... Just said what the midwife said. 'Bout how it could go past twenty-five, thirty weeks. Right up to the birth in some –

RACHEL. Sophie!

SOPHIE. I know, I know... I just... I thought... 'Cause she went through it so recently with her Oscar. And she was so excited about the baby. We were chatting and... She's so lovely. Like my work mum!

RACHEL. Give over, Soph. She's a bloody user.

It's discrimination this. With you being pregnant.

We'll call up *Hull Daily Mail*. Do a smacked-bum-face picture for the front page.

She can't get away with it.

SOPHIE. I'm zero hours. She can do what she likes.

RACHEL. I'll call her. Snotty Helen. Do you want me to call her? I'll call her. Tell her how bloody lucky she is to have you. How much of a geek you are – all them qualifications, level two, level three. All them brilliant courses. Giving up all your spare time...

And you're such a natural with the kiddies as well. I'll bloody tell her that and all.

How dedicated.

Tell how much you need this money...

Being serious, you want me to call, I'll call her.

SOPHIE. I'm the worst mum. I'm shit, I'm shit. I hate myself. She's not even here yet and I'm just... I'm shit!

RACHEL. Hey, no, no. This int your fault!

SOPHIE. I haven't been eating.

RACHEL. What?

SOPHIE. I haven't had the money.

RACHEL. But… you're pregnant.

SOPHIE. I know!

I kept thinking, you know, when I get paid, next time I get paid, but my hours keep being cut and cut and –

RACHEL. What do you mean?

Not eating?

Why dint you tell me? Why wunt you tell me, summat like that?

SOPHIE. You told me not to take your food!

RACHEL. What? But I dint… You dint tell me you want earning. I dint know! Soph, if you told me that, honestly, I wunt never of –

How long's this been going on, Sophie?

SOPHIE. Um… few weeks.

RACHEL. Weeks!

SOPHIE. I know. Please, really don't. I know. Did that course, didn't I? Foetal development. Did about how… When pregnant women don't eat properly. Birth defects, prematurity… Just… never… Oh God. Never thought it'd be me.

RACHEL. Why the hell dint you tell me?

SOPHIE. Things haven't exactly been… with us.

RACHEL. Oh Soph…

What about your nan? You tell her?

SOPHIE. No! It just… It sounds so bad! I didn't want her to think I was like…

RACHEL. What? Like me?

SOPHIE. Please, Mum, I need you.

I can't stop thinking… all day, I'm tryna concentrate at work but I'm just thinking… what am I doing to the baby?

Like, is this why she's small for her dates?

RACHEL. No… Darling…

SOPHIE. It's my fault! It's all my fault!

RACHEL. Oh Soph… I'm sorry. I'm so so sorry.

SOPHIE. You was right.

RACHEL. What?

SOPHIE. I can't do this. You was right.

RACHEL. No! I dint mean –

SOPHIE. I can't do this. And now it's too late. Twenty-five weeks, that's too late. I googled it, you know –

RACHEL. Oh Sophie –

SOPHIE. Shouldn't be doing that, should I? Googling it. What kind of mum does that make me…?

But yeah, it's too late. It's just happening. I can't get off. And I can't do it.

RACHEL. You listen here, alright?

You're talking like you're ready to pop. Got three and a half months till baby comes along. Loads of time to get things sorted.

Now, come on. How um…

How about you give me that, hm? And I make you some eggy bread, yeah?

We'll sort it.

Quit stressing.

Yeah?

Scene Four

Twenty-Five Weeks Pregnant

Time: 7 p.m.

RACHEL *sits on the sofa with her head in her hands.*

LINDA *walks in from the bedroom.*

LINDA. She's having a little lie-down on our bed. Don't get
    worked up.

RACHEL. I'm not, I'm not! Course she can!

    My fault this, int it? I mean, she couldn't tell me. Got herself
    in that state. And she couldn't even come to me.

LINDA. Well…

RACHEL. Here it comes. Go on. Get your little black book
    out. Rachel Bielby's *Crimes and Misdemeanours*, Volume
    Forty-One.

LINDA. Actually, I was going to say, last time I looked you
    weren't some head-up-her-backside employer, who is,
    excuse my French, screwing over a pregnant girl in case
    God-forbid she might call in sick.

    So no, I know you think everything revolves around you, but
    in this instance, I don't think it is your fault.

RACHEL. Thanks? I think.

LINDA. What is it you call her? Snobby Helen?

RACHEL. Snotty.

LINDA. If I saw her, I'd very much like to, what was it you
    used to say, Rachel? Put her face back on the wrong way.

    RACHEL *and* LINDA *share a cautious smile.*

    Beat.

RACHEL. Mam…

LINDA. What?

RACHEL. Look, I've never asked you for owt.

LINDA. Except when you walked out and left me with your…

RACHEL. We've done that.

LINDA. And all that time I spent trying to help you do your homework, revise for your exams. Could have sat that English GCSE myself.

RACHEL. Okay –

LINDA. And those nights when you'd go gadding off to Spiders. I'd be calling the police, worried sick, at half-four in the morning, thinking I was going to end up doing a reconstruction on *Crimewatch*. All the while you're merrily sleeping out under the flyover, smoking the 'wacky baccy' with a load of –

RACHEL. This side of the millennium.

LINDA. Well.

RACHEL. Soph's gonna need your help.

LINDA. I know. Should see my 'Google Calendar'. Splashing Ducks, wriggling… baby rumba-zumba…

RACHEL. That's if she gets any work though.

LINDA. Hm.

RACHEL. It is great, Mam. That you're doing all that. It is.

Beat.

But I'm only just breaking even as it is.

LINDA. Oh. I see.

RACHEL. Not a lot. Just so I can get her a couple of Aldi shops. Get her eating right. For the baby.

LINDA. I'm sorry.

RACHEL. You're seriously gonna sit here and do nowt for your granddaughter to spite me?

LINDA. Oh, here we go.

RACHEL. She thinks the bloody world shines out your arse. But you can't spare her twenty quid.

LINDA. Roll up, ladies and gentlemen. There's about to be a performance.

RACHEL. I did what I did, alright? Twenty-odd years ago and I've spent the last two decades tryna prove to you –

LINDA. Not everything's about you, Rachel.

RACHEL. No, it's about Sophie!

LINDA. I've got problems of my own.

RACHEL. Really?

Beat.

Mam?

LINDA. Of course, if I could… I haven't got nothing to give her. I'm sorry. Been living off my post office account last few months but now that's all but gone.

RACHEL. You dint say.

LINDA. I don't like to be a bother. But, in truth, God knows what I'm going to do.

RACHEL. Don't say that.

LINDA. You really think I'd be stopping here if I had a choice? More pots in that sink than Wetherspoon's.

RACHEL. But you're… You're only here till your leg gets better. Then you'll go back to the flat.

LINDA. Landlord threw me out. Couldn't make last month's rent. The shame of it. Sixteen years I've been there.

RACHEL. But when you get back to work you can get another place?

LINDA.…

RACHEL. Mam? I don't… Tell me I don't live with my mother.

LINDA. I can't go back.

RACHEL. What?

LINDA. Don't, because the idea of Imogen making a pig's ear of my chilled section…

But sooner or later, you have to be honest with yourself. Only reason they put her on my section was because I wasn't stacking all my crates before delivery. Which is not me, it's not.

RACHEL. So what? You're not reaching your PB…

LINDA. It's not just that.

RACHEL. Yeah?

LINDA. My leg keeps giving up on me. Was before the fall. And it jumps all night long, like it's got a mind of its own.

RACHEL. I know. I share a bloody bed with you.

LINDA. Rachel, you remember, don't you?

RACHEL. Mam…

LINDA. My mam's funny leg.

RACHEL. There's a million things that could be. Pulled muscle. Arthritis…

LINDA. Rachel, it's the Parkinson's, I know it is.

RACHEL. They told you that?

LINDA. Don't go telling our Sophie. She's got enough on her plate.

RACHEL. Mam.

LINDA. Promise me.

RACHEL. Yeah. Course. What've they told you?

LINDA. They've referred me. Got an appointment on the second with the neurologist. Wouldn't do that, would they? Refer me. If it was all in my head.

RACHEL. You're jumping the gun. Come on, let's just see what they say.

LINDA. I always thought I'd do something.

RACHEL. What?

LINDA. Oh I don't know. It's always changing. Every year, since I left school, I've gone into WHSmith on the third of January, bought a diary, and jotted down all these extraordinary... unexpected things. Back when I was at Marks, promotion to the Beverley branch. Then learn Mandarin. Go on *Pointless*. Pathetic. When you say it out loud.

RACHEL. So why dint you do them?

LINDA. Here we go.

RACHEL. What?

LINDA. Some people might be able to go off when they want, snog who they want –

RACHEL. Course, hant seen you in years but it's still my fault.

LINDA. But I had a daughter about to hit self-destruct. A mother I had to get up to turn three times a night. Had to keep pushing the other stuff deep down inside me. And now it's too late.

Beat.

RACHEL. But if it is... Dunt have to stop you. I mean Nana Joan had me jealous of her social life. Her jazz dance, Highland dance, sword dance...

LINDA. Egyptian belly dance.

RACHEL. Exactly!

So... 'Cause you're getting ahead of yourself but if it is... Dunt have to hold you back. Whatever it is you wanna... Even more reason to go for it.

Beat.

And if... You know, at some point, you need a bit of extra support...

I'll see you right.

Owe you, don't I? For those *Jane Eyre* essays and the 'wacky baccy'.

I'm saying I'll... look after you or whatever.

LINDA. I can't think of anything worse.

RACHEL *can't help laughing*.

RACHEL *squeezes* LINDA*'s hand*.

Scene Five

Twenty-Eight Weeks Pregnant

Time: 6 p.m.

SOPHIE *on the sofa*.

RACHEL *on the phone*.

RACHEL. Yeah, so could you tell her I can't make it again
tonight? Aw don't, Trace, tell me about it. Been weeks since
I properly engaged my core.

Shuffles forward – away from SOPHIE.

Yeah well I'm doing George again, aren't I?

George down De La Pole. Yeah. He's alright. Can get a bit
messy. Between you and me I reckon he's a two-woman job.

SOPHIE *– listening in – retches*.

Oh yeah, you'd know!

Alright, Trace, well I'll let you go.

RACHEL *picks up a bag*.

SOPHIE. Out again?

RACHEL. Yeah. Yeah. I gotta… Yeah.

Now, I er, done you dippy egg and soldiers. Anaemic toast,
just how you like.

SOPHIE. Oh.

RACHEL. They was giving away some bits at work. Sell-by
was yesterday but it's all good stuff.

You wanting owt else before I go? How's about a milky hot choc?

SOPHIE. What? No, I'm alright.

Feeling a bit…

RACHEL. Oh love. Feel crap leaving you. Nan'll be back soon though.

Gimme a smile before I go.

Smile, big smile, proper one.

That's it.

SOPHIE. Mum, can you…?

RACHEL. Yeah, whatever you want.

SOPHIE. Could you stay?

RACHEL. Oh…

SOPHIE. Please.

RACHEL. I'm sorry. Not tonight.

RACHEL hovers, like she's about to hug SOPHIE.

But then awkwardly leaves.

SOPHIE is left alone.

She goes on Facebook. Reads.

SOPHIE. Oh no!

She gets up and starts shoving the Deluxe Snuggle Pod into a bin bag.

No, no, no!

LINDA enters.

LINDA. Blooming heck, Soph, know your mum's been doing your head in but you didn't have to do away with her!

SOPHIE. Oh, um, Nan, there you… Has your phone been off? Just, I've been calling you all day.

LINDA. 'Do away with her'! What am I like?

SOPHIE. Nan, are you drunk?

LINDA. Might of had a Cinzano or two. What's all this?

SOPHIE. It's um… It's a Deluxe Snuggle Pod. The work girls all clubbed together for it. 'Cause it's meant to be like this super-safe co-sleeper. Like it's got a three-hundred-and-sixty-degree air-flow…

But I just saw this thing on Facebook about how this baby fell out of one. And I can't believe I was actually gonna use it, I'm so stupid!

LINDA. Can't believe everything you read on Facebook.

SOPHIE. Yeah, yeah, maybe you're right. We can ask on Monday.

LINDA. Monday?

SOPHIE. Midwife appointment.

LINDA. I'm afraid I might be a teeny bit double-booked.

SOPHIE. What? Oh.

Not being… But could you rearrange?

LINDA. And also, I may not be able to spend quite as much time looking after the baby as I first mentioned.

SOPHIE. No… Nan, you promised! I can't afford childcare! I won't be able to work!

I'm not being… But you said. You've been saying for months.

LINDA. I had a doctor's appointment, today.

SOPHIE. Oh. God. Was it…? It was bad news?

LINDA. I don't know.

SOPHIE. What?

LINDA. I don't know. I didn't go.

Got the bus to Castle Hill but there was this… open-day thingy at the university. So I, honestly, Sophie, this is so unlike me, I just got off.

Didn't know what to do at first. Just wandered round. And then this woman on one of the stalls, she says to me, 'Are you a prospective student?'

Me! 'Prospective student'! Fancy that.

Applied right there and then for the LLB Honours law foundation year! They'll cover it all, fees, maintenance loan. And with any luck I'll be dead before they come wanting the repayments.

Monday's my interview.

SOPHIE. So…?

LINDA. Just imagine it, Sophie, me, sitting in the little café on campus with my notepad. Having big meaty seminar discussions about 'ethics' and 'legislation'. Getting ten per cent NUS discount in Wallis!

I'm going to be the first in the family to go to university!

SOPHIE. I don't understand. Law?

LINDA. I know! Clearly all that *Judge Judy*'s paid off. She said I sounded like I had a 'real aptitude'.

And I should thank you and all. Making me watch *Legally Blonde*.

SOPHIE. You hated *Legally Blonde*.

LINDA. Exactly. Thought to myself, if that tacky bimbo can do it then why can't I?

SOPHIE. Nan… I'm happy for you, I am. It sounds great. But is there a chance…?

LINDA. Not sounding all that happy.

SOPHIE. Could you maybe defer?

LINDA. Been deferring my whole life.

SOPHIE. Or do it part-time?

LINDA. Sophie…

SOPHIE. Girls at work have done it, splitting it over five, six years.

LINDA. I... I can't.

SOPHIE. Why?

LINDA. I thought you'd be made up for me! Out of everyone, honestly, I was most excited to tell you.

SOPHIE. I am, I just... don't know what I'm going to do.

LINDA. Well I'm sorry, Sophie. I am. But to be frank with you, this is my time.

SOPHIE. How can you say that?

LINDA. Come on, that's not you. Palming your responsibilities off on other people.

   You aren't your mam.

SOPHIE. That's not what I'm doing! You said you wanted to help!

LINDA. You wouldn't want me anyway.

SOPHIE. Of course I do.

LINDA. You wouldn't. I... If I'm honest, I was useless. With your mam. With you.

SOPHIE. You're just saying that.

LINDA. I never knew what I was doing. In the first month my stitches got infected, Rachel had colic and screamed whenever I put her down, my nipples got so sore with the breastfeeding I cried through every feed...

   And they always said it'd get better. 'This stage is the hardest.' But I'd get bored stiff playing mums and dads. Or I'd got into school to sort out her tiffs with her mates and make everything ten times worse. Even now I rub her up the wrong way.

SOPHIE. No one finds it easy.

LINDA. It was more than that!

SOPHIE. Nan, please, if you do this, I'll be around, give you
    advice. I'm a childcare professional. Both of us, we can –

LINDA. I had your bag packed.

SOPHIE. What?

LINDA. When I had you, them six weeks.

SOPHIE. Bag?

LINDA. Your mam'd left. No warning.

    And if I'm honest, I understood it. Her going. When your
    mum was little, I'd just lost my Dave and I felt like I was
    living someone else's life but no one gave me the manual.

    And when she... It all started coming back. Those feelings...

    So I packed up a bag of all your little things, ready for the
    Social.

    Beat.

SOPHIE. The Social. You mean...?

LINDA. I thought it'd be best. For you, getting a proper family.
    And for her and all. It takes it out of you, being a mam. It
    chips away. And Rachel hadn't even had a chance to work out
    who she was. This way, I thought, this way she can go back to
    school, carry on with her studies, maybe see something of the
    world. Settle down when she's ready. But it was fine –

SOPHIE. Tell me, please, tell me I've got the wrong end of the
    stick, 'cause...

LINDA. No, no it was fine, wasn't it? Because she came back
    and she took you –

SOPHIE. You were going to get rid of me?

LINDA. Marks were about to let me go. I was in a spin. I was
    wrong, I can see now.

SOPHIE. Why the hell are you telling me this now?

LINDA. Look, I'm excited to meet the baby, I am, I just can't
    be there all the time.

SOPHIE. Get out.

LINDA. Where am I meant to go?

SOPHIE. I don't care.

LINDA. Come on, no, Sophie, Sophie.

SOPHIE. I just want to be on my own.

LINDA. I'm sorry. Really.

LINDA leaves.

SOPHIE is left completely alone.

She holds her bump and cries.

In the silence she talks to the baby.

SOPHIE. I'm sorry. I'm so sorry. Sorry I thought… Why did
I think I could do this? Shit mum. Shit nan. Just this line
of… shit. Why did I think I could be a good mum?

I can't sleep at night. 'Cause all I can think is you… What
I've done to you. Close my eyes and every time you're
getting smaller and smaller… See you shrinking inside o'me.
See your skin wrinkling. Bagging off you. Happening that
fast I can't stop it. On fast-forward. Close my eyes – every
time – you've shrunk that bit more. Know one day I'm
gonna shut my eyes and you won't be… won't…

Think 'bout money… Think 'bout money… Count it…
Recount it… Draw out figures on the shower door on
a morning. Case there's summat I've missed.

Look at other mums. All the time. Looking at other mums.
Proper mums. On the bus, on Instagram, at work – when
I actually get any work.

Think 'bout how much better your life would be if you was
theirs, not mine. Their daughter'd be plumptious and gorgeous
and flourishing. Not 'small for dates'. Their daughter…

'I really think I can be a good mum.' God. God.

Wanna punch my head in…

If I could I would…

Punch and punch all the fucking teeth outta my skull…

For thinking…

For not…

Not getting…

Forgetting…

Forgetting…

I'm just too broken to be someone's mum.

Beat.

No. No… No… No no no.

Mum!

She touches her thigh – she's bleeding.

I'm bleeding!

God, this is my fault.

It's my fault.

MUM!

SOPHIE *tries calling* RACHEL *on the phone.*

No answer.

Tries again.

MUM!

Help me.

This is my fault. It's my fault.

Help. I need help. I'm bleeding.

Please.

MUM!

Oh God. God this is all my… It's my fault.

Please.

MUM!

MUM!

Scene Six

Twenty-Eight Weeks Pregnant

Time: 3 a.m.

SOPHIE, *home from hospital, faces* RACHEL.

RACHEL. But they said everything was fine.

SOPHIE. Not the point.

RACHEL. I'm just saying, that's all. I don't get why you've got a right face on when they said it was all clear.

SOPHIE. 'Cause that's not the point!

RACHEL. Ugh, Sophie. You know half the time...

SOPHIE. Nan'd pissed off. Left me.

RACHEL. Yeah well you don't wanna go being too hard on her.

SOPHIE. What?

RACHEL. Nowt. Just... Alright, I'm sorry I want there.

SOPHIE. And where were you? Sucking off some pervert from Tinder?

What is wrong with this family?

RACHEL. Sophie!

SOPHIE. I thought I was losing her. I dint know if I was gonna give birth to a premature baby, or a baby that was... I dint know what was...

And you just let me go through all that, on my own. What
sort of a mum does that make you?

RACHEL. Well, sorry but –

SOPHIE. 'But'? Are you joking?

RACHEL. It int like I can just follow you round though, is it?
You know, all the time. Go to work with you. Sleep next to
you. Sit with you while you have a slash. Supervise you
twenty-four-seven. You're a grown bloody woman, Soph –

SOPHIE. Could of at least had your phone on!

RACHEL. I couldn't of known that –

SOPHIE. But no, obviously you wanna pretend like your
pregnant daughter doesn't exist –

RACHEL. Look, I'm sorry you was scared and I want there,
obviously I am, but…

Yeah, I'm sorry.

SOPHIE. You're unbelievable.

RACHEL. Taking yourself to hospital in a cab, that's shit. So,
yeah, sorry. I don't know how much more I can –

SOPHIE. Not just last night though, is it? Been running out on
me your whole life.

RACHEL. Told you! I want well. Hardly knew who I was.
I wunt of done that to you, not ever, if I want poorly. Soph,
you know that, yeah? You've got to know that.

SOPHIE. Dunno. Dunno really. 'Cause it kinda feels like
you've enjoyed getting rid of me these last few years and all.

RACHEL. What you on about?

SOPHIE. Oh come on, my eighteenth birthday, feels like you
went, 'That's it now. I'm free. Thank God.' Minute the
door closed you was moving into a one-bed flat, putting on
a bodycon dress and getting hammered –

RACHEL. It want like that.

SOPHIE. Just pathetically tryna go back to when you were a teenager – before you found out you were having me, when you was stoned out your mind and your life was perfect.

RACHEL. Sophie, if you think that's how –

SOPHIE. I thought, I really thought, moving in here. We could go back to how things was. Everything what came up, us going through it – together.

RACHEL. I've been busy –

SOPHIE. Yeah, you've got better things to do. You have no idea how shit I feel every single day. And I'm just alone with all of it.

RACHEL. And what about me?

SOPHIE. What about 'you'?

RACHEL. Minute you turned eighteen you had your pennies saved up. After all I did for you. All I give up –

SOPHIE. Oh my God.

RACHEL. 'Need my own space.' Like living with me was some kinda juvenile sentence. 'Need my own space.' So you pissed off to a houseshare with six strangers.

And then there's me. Knowing all the time you was ten minutes down the road but I had to wait a fortnight for a phone call.

SOPHIE. Aw come on. I had my job. First time I had girls from work asking if I wanted to go ATIK on a weekend… That was… After what… With school… That was massive for me, you know that. You can't make me feel bad for not –

RACHEL. Yeah but all my life. All my adult life, all I was was somebody's mam, want I? And then you left and who the hell was I?

Eighteen years I hant dated. Dint have no friends 'cept mums what talked about mum things. But I dint have any mum things to talk about no more, did I?

I only had work to get up for. Evenings, weekends I just laid in bed. Whole weekends. Not showering. Eating a pile of shit – or not eating at all. For months. This needy-no-longer-mam, just waiting for you to call to ask how to use a washer.

And then I realised… it was over. You dint need me no more. So I moved to a cheaper place, put some lippy on, got myself on the apps, went 'I aren't dead, I'm hardly thirty, I'm gonna get myself my own bloody life.'

SOPHIE. God, I honestly can't believe you're making this about you after you left me –

RACHEL. I was working.

SOPHIE. What?

RACHEL. Last night. When you called.

SOPHIE. …I don't understand. Working?

RACHEL. Got a gig as a home-carer, doing five or six people a night. Trace from Pole said they had extra shifts going at her place. Just temporary cover so…

SOPHIE. But… What? What? No, you was out with some 'George'…

RACHEL. George, yeah. One of the old boys. He's alright, you know. Flatterer, and his banter's on point…

SOPHIE. Since when you been doing this??

RACHEL. Since you told me you want eating.

Did wanna tell you 'cause I dint want you getting your hopes up. They want you when they want you sorta thing. Hundred and thirty-five quid a week some weeks though, Soph.

Enough to cover some of the hours you're losing. For now.

I'm gonna go out, when I get paid, gonna get you all the bits you need for your hospital bag. And then we can start putting a bit by, eh? Little bank of savings. Take the pressure off you.

SOPHIE. Mum… Oh my God… I don't… I really don't know what to…

So… are you still doing full-time at school? And the cleaning before and after?

RACHEL. Oh here she goes.

SOPHIE. What?

RACHEL. Knew you'd be like this. All, 'you're overdoing it'.

SOPHIE. No, I want I just… Are you sure? 'Cause it's a lot, I just don't want…

RACHEL. I'm sure. Hundred per cent. Okay? So quit your whining.

Beat.

They hug.

SOPHIE. Thank you. Thank you thank you. You have no idea how… Honestly, you don't know how much…

RACHEL. Ssh. Ssh. Ssh.

Look, you… You go and get yourself some sleep.

Nah, nah, I mean like, you can… In my bed.

SOPHIE. Thanks, Mum.

SOPHIE *goes to bed.*

RACHEL*'s left alone.*

LINDA *enters.*

LINDA. What's been going on? Got twenty-odd missed calls.

RACHEL. Dunt matter now.

Mam?

LINDA. She's told you.

RACHEL. Yeah.

And I just wanna say –

LINDA. Look, I'm sorry. I am. But I need this. I really need this.

RACHEL. I wanna say good on you.

LINDA. Really?

RACHEL. Hull Uni freshers int gonna know what's hit it.

RACHEL *squeezes* LINDA*'s arm.*

Scene Seven

Forty Weeks (+ Five Days) Pregnant

Time: 1 p.m

RACHEL *lying on the sofa – clearly knackered.*

A big crash.

RACHEL. Bloody… You need a hand?

SOPHIE (*offstage*). No, no, it's okay, you rest up.

Another crash.

RACHEL. You sure you…?

SOPHIE. No, no. I can do it.

RACHEL *notices a present bag next to the sofa, she opens it.*

SOPHIE (*very, very pregnant*) *drags out the crib.*

RACHEL. What the hell is this?

SOPHIE. Oh. Nan brought it round.

RACHEL *holds up the present – a 'Future Student of Hull University'-branded baby vest.*

She also asked if you got tickets yet for her Drama Soc production of *Sweeney Todd.*

RACHEL. Think I'm already booked in to scratch my own eyes out.

She turns to the crib.

Anyway. What d'you think of this, will it do?

SOPHIE. Yeah, yeah, it's really –

RACHEL. I mean, it int no Deluxe Snuggle Pod –

SOPHIE. No, no, Mum it's… It's perfect.

RACHEL. I mean, don't be expecting her to be doing any
    sleeping in it mind. You can kiss them eight hours goodbye.

SOPHIE. If she ever actually comes out.

RACHEL. You alright?

SOPHIE. Yeah.

RACHEL. Soph…

SOPHIE. If I say it, it's gonna sound stupid.

RACHEL. Wunt be the first time.

SOPHIE. I just keep thinking, what if like… What if after
    everything, what if she's late 'cause she doesn't wanna
    come out?

RACHEL. Yeah, you're right. That does sound stupid.

SOPHIE. Mum!

Beat.

RACHEL. You er… settled on a name for her yet?

SOPHIE. What?

RACHEL. A name.

SOPHIE. Oh, um, I thought… Lily. Lily Anthea.

RACHEL. Lily?

SOPHIE. Yeah.

RACHEL. Not 'Hortensia'?

SOPHIE. I just though it sounded sophisticated! It was only on the shortlist!

Beat.

RACHEL. Y'alright, Lily?

SOPHIE. What?

RACHEL. Shut it. I'm talking to my granddaughter.

Honestly. Sorry, Lily. So anyway, I'm your granny. Er but I'm a very very young granny. You'll probably get a lotta schoolfriends asking, 'Is that your mam?' Or, you know, more like a much-older half-sister. That probably will happen.

Er, and this is your mam. She's alright.

'Cause God knows, it's a shit-scary business, this parenting lark. I mean, seriously, Lil, before your mam come along –

SOPHIE. Yeah, yeah.

RACHEL. I'm just saying, Lily… Before she come along, I never gave a shit about anything. Teachers'd wanna bash my head against a table 'cause I want actually stupid, I just dint care enough to try. Other girls'd be staying in all weekend over their books. But me? Nah.

Same with jobs, Lil. I'd roll in, late and hungover. I just couldn't ever make myself feel owt when the bosses told me I was fired. Same with blokes, mates… my mam.

I never worried about owt, never felt guilty. Honestly my head was that far up my arse, it was like I was dead inside.

Then, don't tell your mam this, Lily, but then she comes along and all of a sudden I'm terrified. All the time. First time I changed her nappy, I cut her out her little vest with scissors I was that scared of making a mistake. Of snapping her little legs and arms.

Never had it before. This, fear, all the time. Was scared to do anything 'cause I was sure whatever I did, it was gonna be wrong. And sometimes it was. Is.

But that want ever 'cause I dint love her, Lily. It want never, never that. Was 'cause I thought she deserved the best mam in the world. But see, that's where you're alright, Lil. 'Cause you've got the best bloody mam in the world.

SOPHIE....

RACHEL. What?

SOPHIE....

RACHEL. What?

SOPHIE. I... I love you, Mum. You know that? I love you.

RACHEL. Yeah, well, love you and all, don't I?

SOPHIE. We gonna be alright?

RACHEL *kisses* SOPHIE.

Argh. Fuck. Sorry. Ooh.

RACHEL. Soph?

Sophie what's...?

Come on, use your words.

What's happening?

SOPHIE. I think... Mum, I think this is...

RACHEL. And you're a hundred per cent it int just a fart this time?

SOPHIE. Arghhhh!

RACHEL. Fuck!

The End.

www.nickhernbooks.co.uk

facebook.com/nickhernbooks

twitter.com/nickhernbooks